Copyright 2021 by Dr. Archibald Jc

This document is geared towards providing exact and reliable information in regard to the topic and issue covered. The publication is sold on the idea that the publisher is not required to render an accounting, officially permitted, or otherwise, qualified services. If advice is necessary, legal or professional, a practiced individual in the profession should be ordered. From a Declaration of Principles which was accepted and approved equally by a Committee of the American Bar Association and a Committee of Publishers and Associations. In no way is it legal to reproduce, duplicate, or transmit any part of this document by either electronic means or in printed format. Recording of this publication is strictly prohibited and any storage of this document is not allowed unless with written permission from the publisher. All rights reserved. The information provided herein is stated to be truthful and consistent, in that any liability, in terms of inattention or otherwise, by any usage or abuse of any policies, processes, or Directions: contained within is the solitary and utter responsibility of the recipient reader. Under no circumstances will any legal responsibility or blame be held against the publisher for any reparation, damages, or monetary loss due to the information herein, either directly or indirectly. By continuing with this book, readers agree that the author is under no circumstances responsible for any losses, indirect or direct, that are incurred as a result of the information presented in this document, including, but not limited to inaccuracies, omissions and errors. Respective authors own all copyrights not held by the publisher. The information herein is offered for informational purposes solely and is universal as so. The presentation of the information is without a contract or any type of guarantee assurance. The information herein is offered for informational purposes solely and is universal as so. The presentation of the information is without contract or any type of guarantee assurance. Readers acknowledge that the author is not engaging in the rendering of legal, financial, medical or professional advice. Please consult a licensed professional before attempting any techniques outlined in this book.

CONTENTS

INTRODUCTION 5
BENEFITS OF A BLAND DIET 6
BLAND DIET: WHAT'S IN, WHAT'S OUT? 8
    Vegetables and Fruits 8
    Milk and Dairy Products 10
    Bread and Grains 11
    Proteins 12
    Fats and Oils 13
    Beverages and Other Food Items 14
RISKS AND COMPLAINTS 15
TIPS AND TRICKS 16
APPETIZER RECIPES 18
        Kale & Cheese Omelette 19
        Scrambled Eggs 21
        Apricots & Quinoa Porridge 23
        Frittata with Leafy Greens 25
        Cherry Rye French Toast 28
        Berry Pancakes 30
        Spinach Papaya Superfood Smoothie 33
        Fruity and Healthy Barley 35
        Banana Pancakes 37
        Savory Potato Fries 39

    Greens Muffins 41

    Tofu Quesadilla 43

MAIN MEALS 45

    Turkey Soup with Tarragon 46

    Acorn Squash Risotto 49

    Green Onion & Quinoa Soup 52

    Marjoram & Lime Lamb Soup 54

    Greens Soup 56

    Carrot Soup 58

    Green Beans Risotto 60

    Seafood Chowder 62

    Roast Turkey 64

    Beef and Vegetable Soup 67

    Pumpkin Soup 69

    Sweet Potato & Thyme Risotto 71

    Coconut Parsnips Soup 74

    Baked Salmon with Quinoa 76

DESSERT RECIPES 78

    Almond Barley Pudding 79

    Plantain Baked 81

    Sweet Potato Scones 83

    Dairy-Free Rice Pudding 85

    Banana Quinoa 87

    Pumpkin Bread Pudding 89

- Coconut Avocado Pudding ... 91
- Yogurt Biscuits ... 93
- Pumpkin Pie Quinoa Pudding ... 95
- Granola ... 97
- Coconut Lemon Cake ... 99
- Dulce de Leche Cookies ... 101

SMOOTHIES AND DRINKS ... 104
- Banana Almond Smoothie ... 105
- Plantains & Orange Smoothie ... 107
- Chocolate Coconut Smoothie ... 109
- Apple Pie Smoothie ... 111
- Avocado Smoothie ... 113
- Healthy Shamrock Shake ... 115
- Hot Chocolate ... 117
- Apple Compote Smoothie ... 119
- Cantaloupe Smoothie ... 121
- Chai Tea Smoothie ... 123
- Ginger Butter Squash Latte ... 125
- Red Velvet Smoothie ... 127

2-WEEKS MEAL PLAN ... 129
- 1st Week Meal Plan ... 130
- 2nd Week Meal Plan ... 131

INTRODUCTION

Our digestive system is in charge of turning food into energy and removing waste from our bodies. Given the amount of work and food the digestive system must process, it may encounter challenges that affect its operations and, as a result, the overall health of the body.

Constipation, intestinal inflammation, bloating, diverticulitis, acid-peptic illness and acid reflux are just a few of the digestive disorders that might develop. When such serious issues occur, doctors advise giving the digestive system adequate time to relax without neglecting the body's need for nutrients. This can be achieved by following an eating plan called a bland diet. It is a diet that excludes fibrous, raw, spicy and fatty food, as well as food that is hard to digest. However, this does not imply that a bland diet merely supports the consumption of a limited variety of foods. This book will introduce you to a plethora of healthy, nutritious and delicious recipes, which will make your life and diet easier.

BENEFITS OF A BLAND DIET

The sole purpose of a bland diet is to fight the symptoms of distorted digestive organs, reduce discomfort and provide an individual with all necessary nutrition their body needs to survive.

A bland diet is commonly advised to people with digestive concerns or diseases. Foods in this diet help ease intestinal irritations due to nausea, diarrhea, changes in taste, loss of appetite, acid reflux, heartburn, gastroesophageal reflux disease (GERD), ulcers, and gastrointestinal infections. It is also prescribed to patients with diverticulosis - the development of small pouches in the digestive tract - and to those with diverticulitis - the infection or inflammation of the pouches. Likewise, this diet is advised to patients who will undergo digestive or colonic procedures like colonoscopy.

As a type of eating plan, a bland diet also offers unique advantages to men and women. Aside from helping you lose a lot of weight by eliminating fatty, processed, spicy, and difficult-to-digest foods, this diet will also help you fight overeating, a feeling of fullness, and constipation, as well as help you build healthier day to day eating habits. While on a bland diet, the digestive tract is given adequate time to break down and absorb the nutrients from the meals one eats because the diet entails eating smaller meals, eating slowly, and avoiding lying down straight after meals. Furthermore, this diet may reduce the amount of acids in your stomach and prevent potential damage to your intestinal flora and organs.

Another advantage of this diet is that it makes the stool firmer and helps to replace the nutrients lost by the body as a result of the aforementioned disorders, allowing the body to return to its normal activities.

Although a bland diet is not a permanent treatment, it can help prevent the development of or exacerbation of different digestive issues. Though it is most advantageous to people who fight digestive disorders and discomforts, this diet might also come in handy to individuals who are thinking about replacing their diet with a healthier option or wish to lose some weight. However, before modifying a daily food plan, one should consult with their doctor or ensure that it meets their nutritional needs.

BLAND DIET: WHAT'S IN, WHAT'S OUT?

Once you begin this diet, the three key qualities of food that you must keep in mind are: the food should be low in fiber, low in fat, and easy to digest. While most diets involve fruits and vegetables, many of them will be avoided because they contain too much fiber. This diet also avoids the use of strong spices, tastes, and heavy seasonings, leaving the rest bland and almost unpalatable.

Vegetables and Fruits

Vegetables included in a bland diet should be, in general, cooked until very soft, pureed, or juiced for faster consumption and absorption. Fruits should also be served in the form of purees or juices but have to be diluted in order to separate the pulp or fibers from the extracts. Skins and seeds shall not be absorbed as they are the most fibrous part of the fruit and are harder to digest. White and sweet potatoes, squash, pumpkin, and carrots are the most common vegetables included in this diet. To ensure tenderness, they should be cooked skinless. Mashing them before serving reduces the amount of work the digestive system has to do.

In addition, you are encouraged to eat beets, peas, spinach and green beans. Avocados, despite their increased fiber content, may also be tolerated well. Among the fruit, banana and melon, along with the apple sauce, are the best options.

Raw, steamed, blanched, and fried vegetables, as well as fresh, raw, dried and frozen fruits, should be placed aside because they are harder on your digestive system. Among the fruit, you should also avoid all types of fruit with small seeds, such as all berries, grapes, prunes, etc.

To avoid the creation of too much gas in the digestive system, which is known as flatulence, vegetables that can cause it, such as green peppers, cabbage, cucumber, corn, broccoli, Brussels sprouts, and cauliflower, should be avoided.

Finally, even though they are suggested in the diet, tomatoes and citrus fruits, such as lemon, orange, lime, etc., should be avoided if you have hyperacidity, heartburn, or acid reflux – depending on your symptoms.

If the time and effort required to prepare veggies and fruits are a source of concern for you, canned or bottled vegetables and fruits are the ideal options because they are convenient and widely available. However, these should be consumed in moderation because they may contain artificial preservatives and loads of sugar. Choose less sugary or vinegary delights, or create your own batches of canned fruits and veggies.

Milk and Dairy Products

Milk and dairy products are nutrient-dense foods that are, in general, easily digested and absorbed by the body. Given this, they are also included in the bland diet, albeit with a few limits. Dairy products ranging from low-fat to fat-free are all viable possibilities. Low-fat and fat-free milk, low-fat yogurt, and lightly flavored cheeses such as cottage cheese, Leicester, and Swiss cheese are a few great examples. Plant-based milk, such as flax milk, walnut milk, almond milk, soy milk, and coconut milk, are also encouraged, as they are among the healthier dairy alternatives.

However, physicians advise you to be careful when consuming dairy and to control your intake of dairy products. Milk protein and lactose intolerance can produce stomach discomfort for some people. For such people, an absolute absence of dairy from their diet might be advisable, which might aid in the recovery of peptic ulcers. Above mentioned plant-based alternatives might come in handy in such cases.

Full-fat milk and yogurt, fatty dairy meals such as whipped cream and dairy-based ice cream, and strongly flavored cheeses such as Roquefort or

Blue cheese should be avoided since they contain a high percentage of fat and are hard to digest.

Bread and Grains

Keeping track of how your body reacts after consuming gluten-containing grains is a useful habit to develop, especially if you intend to transition to a bland diet. Some people's digestive systems respond negatively to gluten, resulting in worsening their symptoms. In this scenario, gluten-free grains are the best option to overcome the symptoms. Sorghum, quinoa, oats, and brown rice are all great examples.

If gluten does not have a detrimental impact on your system, white bread, seedless rye, or refined wheat items for breakfast or sides are great options. Plain soda crackers, cream of wheat, processed oats, prepared cereals, soft white noodles, low-sugar cold cereals, and crackers are also good options.

On the other hand, high-fiber and whole-grain items shall be avoided. Avoid grain bread made from sprouted wheat, whole-wheat pasta, any fiber-enriched product, such as cereal, as well as any other bread and grain items containing more than five grams of fiber per serving.

Proteins

As previously stated, a bland diet necessitates meals that are low in fat, low in fiber, and easily digestible; however, most protein-rich foods fail to meet one or more of these criteria. Even so, these protein sources can be included in the diet by putting in extra work and time during preparation.

Frying is not an option when it comes to cooking these types of dishes. Poultry and meats such as chicken, turkey, beef, and lamb can be included in your meal plan if roasted or baked without the skin. Aside from cooking them thoroughly and ensuring softness, these methods drain extra fat. However, for optimal flavor, you can also remove the skin after cooking prior to consuming.

When choosing meat, try to avoid fatty cuts of beef and poultry, as well as all types of meat that in general include high-fat content, such as pork.

The soft flesh of fish, such as salmon or trout, and shellfish, such as prawns, crabs, and lobsters, do not necessitate the removal of skin or shell. Cooking them with their skin shells will give the dish exquisite flavors. Seafood is a great option because the meat is soft and has an excellent natural flavor, which does not need additional seasoning.

Last but not least, eggs. Eggs are one of the healthiest and most nutrient-dense foods on the market, are also distinguished by their high protein content and a variety of cooking methods. Given this, including eggs in your meal is advisable as long as it is done in moderation and with little to no spice.

Regarding the plant-based alternatives, you may consume tofu, finely mixed peanut butter, and other nut pastes, which are high in protein. As such, pastes are also high in fat; eat them in moderation.

Fats and Oils

Only a few fat and oil sources are allowed in a bland diet. To add flavor to your meals, a drizzle of your preferred healthy oil, like cold press olive oil, peanut oil, coconut, or canola oil, all of them rich in monosaturated fats, will be helpful in reducing the blandness of your meal. Heavily refined oils and fatty products, such as sunflower oil or margarine, on the other hand, should not be consumed.

In addition, adding any fat or oil sources to your dishes should be monitored, so you do not consume too much and further distort your stomach and intestines.

Beverages and Other Food Items

Caffeinated, cream-based, and alcoholic beverages should be avoided while on a bland diet as they further trigger gastrointestinal conditions and irritations.

Physicians emphasized that the most soothing drinks are chamomile tea, green tea, and weak black tea, which can also help flush toxins from the body.

In addition, many sauces and dressings, including mustard, ketchup, salad dressing and horseradish, should be avoided due to the high fat and sugar content. Fat-filled and hard-to-digest treats such as cheesecake, dark chocolate, olives, popcorn, granola, nuts and all strong spices should also be avoided since they might worsen your symptoms.

RISKS AND COMPLAINTS

The bland diet is sometimes regarded as hard and uninteresting because of its constraints, lack of fresh food, aromatic variations and flavors, particularly. An individual's general health could be affected by a long-term bland diet since one might not consume all necessary daily nutrients. For example, fiber has a lot of health advantages. It is efficient in reducing bad cholesterol, maintain blood sugar levels and maintain good intestinal bacteria. Fresh fruit and vegetable, including peels, also include a variety of important vitamins and minerals which get destroyed when cooked. A long-term bland diet, therefore, removes all these important benefits your body needs to function properly.

In addition, fiber and vitamin suppressions could result in constipation, bad skin and hair. Ideally, a person should stay on a bland diet only during recovery from a digestive condition. Once your stomach and intestines have rested, try to transition back to your regular diet plan.

Consulting with your doctor or dietitian about the duration of the diet, as well as the potential impact on your overall health, is highly advisable.

TIPS AND TRICKS

Eating smaller servings several times a day is more convenient for the stomach. Savoring this meal by eating slowly and taking two hours to rest after eating provides enough time for the stomach to digest, absorb, and prepare for your next meal. Also, try to avoid eating at least two hours prior to going to bed so that your food gets digested before you lay down.

During breakfast, a bread's dull taste could be saved by adding spreads, like seedless jams and jellies and creamy nut pastes.

Removing fried, seasoned, cured, dried, and smoked food is also a must-do to maximize the benefits of a bland diet. Foods prepared in such ways do not meet the requirements of a bland diet and are triggers of some irritating digestive issues.

In terms of flavors, mild flavors are encouraged. Too many seasonings may be irritating to the stomach. However, experimenting or interchanging fresh and mild spices like basil, parsley, bay leaf, sea salt, and other mild flavorings are great ways to spice up your meals.

Another method to add flavor to your meal is through marinating, which brings out the natural taste of meat. Fruit juices such as orange juice or pineapple juice are commonly used for marinating chicken meat and pork. You can also mix onions or garlic to your marinade and remove them prior to cooking your meat.

Beverages, including water, should be avoided during meals, for these might fill up your stomach instead of the food that you are eating. This will cause your body to absorb fewer nutrients.

Finally, to avoid getting sick of the same taste, flavor, and meals, planning your meals in advance is effective. Through this, you get a chance to identify which food to retain, try, and substitute. You can also personalize your meal plan, depending on what types of food cause you the most trouble and what not. However, you should consult your plan with your doctor or dietitian.

Last but not least, bad habits such as heavy drinking or smoking are never good for your health. So, try to avoid alcohol and cigarettes as much as possible as they can both increase your stomach acid and cause different troubles, including constipation for some, diarrhea for others, stomach tension and gas.

On the following pages, you will get to know 50 delicious recipe ideas, along with a 2-week diet plan that will help you get your stomach troubles under control. Let's not waste any more time. Dig into it and enjoy!

APPETIZER RECIPES

Kale & Cheese Omelette

Prep time: 10 min   Cook time: 10 min   Servings: 1

Ingredients

- *2 cups kale, rinsed*
- *2 large eggs*
- *1 tsp coconut oil, divided*
- *1 ounce cottage cheese, divided*
- *1 tbsp chopped cilantro*
- *Salt and pepper, to taste*

Directions

- In a saucepan with a lid, add ¼ cup of cold water, a pinch of salt and kale. Cover and cook over medium heat for about 1 to 2 minutes until the kale is tender. Drain as much water as you can and wring it out. Put aside.

- In a medium bowl, mix the eggs with 1 tbsp of water, salt and pepper to taste.
- Heat the oil in a small non-stick skillet over medium heat. Add half of the eggs and cook without stirring until the eggs are set.
- Using a rubber spatula, lift the edges of the omelette and tilt the pan so that the raw eggs run over the edges of the pan and under the omelette.
- Sprinkle half the amount of cheese, wilted kale and cilantro on one side of the omelette. Fold the uncovered side of the omelette over the cheese side. Cook, 1 minute, until the inside of the omelette is set and the cheese begins to melt.
- Serve and enjoy!

NUTRITION FACTS (PER SERVING)

Calories	274	
Total Fat	15g	19%
Saturated Fat	7.4g	37%
Cholesterol	374mg	125%
Sodium	314mg	14%
Total Carbohydrate	15.9g	6%
Dietary Fiber	2.1g	7%
Total Sugars	0.9g	
Protein	20.5g	

Tips: Cook over medium heat. Also consider the size of the pan before you start. If the pan is too large, the tortilla cooks too quickly, and if it is too small, it can only be cooked with a liquid center on the outside. If you are using a small saucepan, try to use no more than two eggs for each omelette.

Scrambled Eggs

| Prep time: 5 min | Cook time: 5 min | Servings: 2 |

Ingredients

- *4 large eggs*
- *¼ cup coconut milk*
- *salt, to taste*
- *fresh herbs to taste (parsley, basil…)*
- *1 tbsp olive oil*

Directions

- Crack the eggs into a glass bowl and beat them until they turn light yellow.
- Add the milk to the eggs and season with salt and fresh herbs. Beat the eggs like crazy. If you're not up to it, you can use an electric mixer or a stand mixer with a whisk. Whichever device you use, try to get as much air as possible into the eggs.

- Preheat a solid-bottomed non-stick skillet over medium-low heat. Add the oil and let it melt.
- When the saucepan is hot enough, pour the eggs into it. Do not stir. Let the eggs cook for up to a minute or until the bottom hardens but does not brown.
- Using a heat-resistant rubber spatula, gently press one the edge of the egg toward the center while tilting the pan to allow the egg, which is still liquid, to sink underneath. Repeat with the other edges until all of the liquid is gone.
- Turn off the heat and keep stirring the egg gently until all the raw parts are firm. Do not break the egg and keep the curd as big as possible. As you add more ingredients, add them quickly.
- Transfer to a plate when the eggs are ready, but still moist and soft. Serve immediately and enjoy.

NUTRITION FACTS (PER SERVING)

Calories	329	
Total Fat	30.7g	39%
Saturated Fat	21.2g	106%
Cholesterol	372mg	124%
Sodium	222mg	10%
Total Carbohydrate	2.5g	1%
Dietary Fiber	0.7g	2%
Total Sugars	1.8g	
Protein	13.3g	

<u>*Tips: Make it easy on yourself and cook your eggs in a non-stick sauté pan. Use a heat-resistant silicone spatula so it doesn't melt or scratch the pan*</u>

Apricots & Quinoa Porridge

| Prep time: 5 min | Cook time: 15 min | Servings: 4 |

Ingredients

- *3 cups coconut milk*
- *1 cup quinoa*
- *4 dried apricots, diced*
- *Toasted sliced almonds*

Directions

- Combine the coconut milk, quinoa, apricots, and a pinch of salt in a small saucepan.
- Bring to a boil then simmer for 10 to 15 minutes.

- Serve warm or at room temperature with freshly sliced apricots (if using) and toasted almonds.

NUTRITION FACTS (PER SERVING)

Calories	589	
Total Fat	45.9g	59%
Saturated Fat	38.4g	192%
Cholesterol	0mg	0%
Sodium	30mg	1%
Total Carbohydrate	41.1g	15%
Dietary Fiber	7.7g	27%
Total Sugars	9.2g	
Protein	10.6g	

<u>Tips: quinoa easy to digest. This recipe is sometimes recommended after vomiting or diarrhea as it provides the body with the necessary nutrients for easier recovery.</u>

Frittata with Leafy Greens

| Prep time: 5 min | Cook time: 15 min | Servings: 2 |

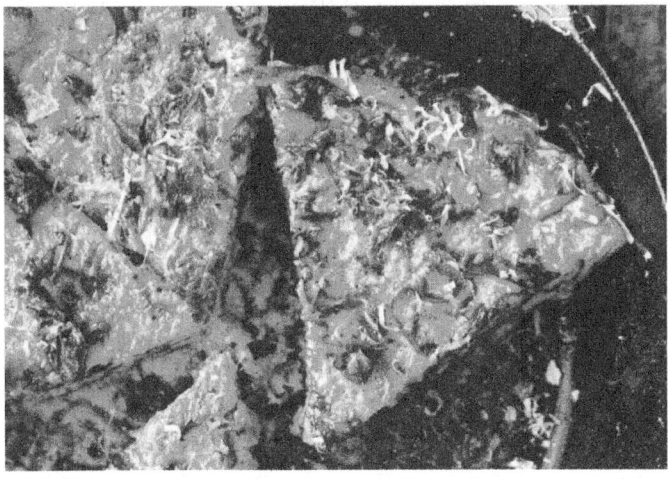

Ingredients

- *½ bunch Swiss chard*
- *2 eggs*
- *1 tbsp chopped leek*
- *1 tbsp coconut oil*
- *1 large onion, peeled, chopped and sliced*
- *1½ tbsp chopped basil*
- *Salt and pepper*

Directions

- Remove the delicate green from the tough stems. Wash the vegetables well.
- Put in a large saucepan with the water glued to the leaves. Sprinkle with salt. Steam until the leaves are wilted and tender. Allow excess moisture to drain off and squeeze out.
- Roughly chop and set aside.
- Beat the eggs in a bowl with salt, pepper and 1 tbsp of water. Add the chopped leek if using. Put aside.
- In a large skillet, slowly sauté the onion in the oil until caramelized and golden brown, 5 to 8 minutes over medium-low heat.
- Increase the heat to medium-high and add the cooked vegetables to the onion. Fry for 2 minutes. Add the basil and sauté to combine.
- Pour the vegetables into the egg mixture and mix well, then return everything to the pot. Smooth with a spatula to form a thin crepe-shaped frittata.
- Cook until the frittata is half cooked and golden brown where it touches the pan. Slide it gently onto a plate, cooked side down.
- Wipe the pan with a piece of greased paper towels. Place the pan with your hand under the plate on the frittata. Turn the plate and pan to transfer the raw side of the frittata to the pan.
- Cook, 1 to 2 minutes, until set.
- Slide the frittata into a serving platter and serve in quarters.

NUTRITION FACTS (PER SERVING)		
Calories	163	
Total Fat	11.3g	15%
Saturated Fat	7.2g	36%
Cholesterol	164mg	55%
Sodium	73mg	3%
Total Carbohydrate	9.7g	4%
Dietary Fiber	2g	7%
Total Sugars	3.7g	
Protein	7.2g	

Tips: This dish is an excellent source of vitamins K, A and C, as well as a good source of magnesium, potassium, iron and fiber.

Cherry Rye French Toast

| Prep time: 5 min | Cook time: 15 min | Servings: 2 |

Ingredients

- *2 rye bread*
- *1 egg*
- *Coconut milk, as needed*
- *Grated mace*
- *1 tsp coconut oil*

Directions

- Place the slices of bread in a baking dish.
- Crack the egg into a 2-cup measuring cup. Add milk for 1 generous cup.
- Add freshly grated mace and beat well.

- Pour the mixture over the bread and allow the bread to absorb the liquid.
- After a few minutes, turn the bread slices over to make sure the bread is evenly moist.
- Grease a pan with butter. Heat over medium to high heat. When the pan is hot and the butter melts and bubbles, place the soaked bread slices in the pan. While baking, pour the rest of the egg mixture over the slices of bread.
- When one side of the bread is ready, turn the slice over and cook the other side until golden brown.

NUTRITION FACTS (PER SERVING)

Calories	73	
Total Fat	3.5g	5%
Saturated Fat	1.7g	9%
Cholesterol	48mg	16%
Sodium	97mg	4%
Total Carbohydrate	6.5g	2%
Dietary Fiber	0.5g	2%
Total Sugars	3.1g	
Protein	4g	

Tips: Rye bread is a type of bread made from different proportions of rye flour. It can be light or dark in color, depending on the type of flour used and the addition of color, and is generally denser than bread made from wheat flour.

Berry Pancakes

| Prep time: 5 min | Cook time: 15 min | Servings: 2 |

Ingredients

- ⅛ cup rye flour
- ¼ cup sorghum flour
- 1 tbsp honey
- 1 tsp baking powder
- ⅛ tsp salt
- 1 large egg
- ¼ cup plain yogurt
- 2 tbsp coconut milk
- 1 tbsp coconut oil, melted

- ¼ tsp lime zest
- ½ tsp vanilla extract
- Butter, for cooking
- ¾ cup frozen or fresh berries

Directions

- In a small bowl, mix or sift the rye flour, sorghum flour, honey, baking powder and salt. Put aside.
- In a medium bowl, combine egg and yogurt. If you are using regular yogurt, add 2 tbsp of milk, and if you are using Greek yogurt, use 4 tbsp of milk. Combine melted coconut oil, lime zest and vanilla extract until smooth.
- Using a spatula or wooden spoon, stir the flour mixture with the wet ingredients until they are just moistened. The dough will be very thick and a bit lumpy.
- Heat a cast iron skillet or griddle over medium heat. Add a little butter to the pan and after boiling and melting, pour about ¼ cup of batter for each pancake. Work in a pile so as not to clutter the pan. Press the berries into the pancakes.
- Bake for about 3 minutes or until the edges of the pancakes look cooked and bubbles form on the top of the pancakes. Flip and cook for another 3 minutes or until golden brown. Repeat with the rest of the dough.

NUTRITION FACTS (PER SERVING)

Calories	271	
Total Fat	14g	18%
Saturated Fat	10.2g	51%
Cholesterol	95mg	32%
Sodium	209mg	9%
Total Carbohydrate	31g	11%
Dietary Fiber	3.8g	13%
Total Sugars	11.6g	
Protein	8.4g	

Tips: Food high in fiber and whole grains should be avoided on a diet low in fiber or residue, sometimes recommended as part of a light diet. Additionally, gluten can be a trigger for some people, so eating gluten free wheat, rye, and barley can be beneficial.

Spinach Papaya Superfood Smoothie

| Prep time: 5 min | Cook time: 0 min | Servings: 8 |

Ingredients

- *8 cups spinach packed*
- *6 cups soy milk*
- *6 cups papaya chunks*
- *1 tsp vanilla extract*

Directions

- Add all ingredients into a blender.
- Blend until smooth and creamy.
- Pour into glasses and enjoy.

NUTRITION FACTS (PER SERVING)

Calories	173	
Total Fat	5.2g	7%
Saturated Fat	0.6g	3%
Cholesterol	0mg	0%
Sodium	127mg	6%
Total Carbohydrate	24.9g	9%
Dietary Fiber	3.8g	14%
Total Sugars	16g	
Protein	8.3g	

<u>*Tips: People who are trying to lose weight often skip their morning meals and eat large amounts between meals. To avoid this, experts recommend smoothies made with excellent fruits and flavors to keep you full for a long time*</u>

Fruity and Healthy Barley

| Prep time: 5 min | Cook time: 15 min | Servings: 2 |

Ingredients

- *1 cup barley*
- *2 cup water*
- *Generous pinch sea salt*
- *½ tbsp figs*
- *½ tbsp blueberries*
- *¼ tsp nutmeg*
- *1 apple*
- *1 tbsp sliced almonds, dry toasted*
- *1 banana, thinly sliced*
- *Coconut milk*

Directions

- Combine the barley, water, salt, figs, blueberries and nutmeg in a saucepan.
- Bring to a boil, stir well then bring the heat to a boil. Cover and cook for about 10 minutes, stirring occasionally the barley to prevent sticking.
- While the barley is cooking, rub the apple with the thickest hole. When the barley is cooked, add the grated apple until everything is combined.
- Cover the heater and turn it off. Let the barley cook for 5 minutes.
- Serve sprinkled with sliced almonds and bananas as well as milk.

NUTRITION FACTS (PER SERVING)

Calories	481	
Total Fat	5.9g	8%
Saturated Fat	2.3g	11%
Cholesterol	0mg	0%
Sodium	21mg	1%
Total Carbohydrate	99.8g	36%
Dietary Fiber	21.1g	75%
Total Sugars	21.6g	
Protein	13.3g	

Tips: Barley is a very healthy grain. It is rich in vitamins, minerals and other beneficial plant compounds. It is also high in fiber, which is responsible for the majority of its health advantages, which range from improved digestion to reduced hunger and weight loss.

Banana Pancakes

Prep time: 5 min   Cook time: 15 min   Servings: 4

Ingredients

- ½ banana, peeled
- 1 egg
- ¼ cup coconut milk
- ¼ cup sorghum flour
- ½ tsp baking powder
- ¼ tsp freshly grated cinnamon
- ½ tbsp currants
- 1 tbsp melted coconut oil
- 1 pinch sea salt

Directions

- Mash ripe banana with a fork.
- Add the egg and enough coconut milk to reach the 1 cup line. Beat until everything is well combined.
- In a large bowl, combine sorghum flour, baking powder and cinnamon. Add the banana mixture, melted coconut oil, and currants.
- Lightly brush a large skillet with butter or oil. Heat over medium heat. Test the temperature of the pot by spraying water on the pot. The water should bubble and evaporate immediately. Add ¼ cup of batter to the pan for each pancake. Cook in batches, don't overfill your pan.
- Cook for about 2 minutes on each side or if bubbles appear on the surface of the pancakes, brown them. Serve immediately with chopped roasted nuts accompanied by maple syrup and butter.

NUTRITION FACTS (PER SERVING)

Calories	115	
Total Fat	7.2g	9%
Saturated Fat	4.4g	22%
Cholesterol	41mg	14%
Sodium	98mg	4%
Total Carbohydrate	11.1g	4%
Dietary Fiber	1.6g	6%
Total Sugars	2.4g	
Protein	2.9g	

Tips: Eggs are a good source of protein in a bland diet, such as baked skinless chicken, low-fat milk and yogurt, and peanut and other nut butters.

Savory Potato Fries

| Prep time: 5 min | Cook time: 20 min | Servings: 4 |

Ingredients

- *2 large potatoes*
- *2 tbsp coconut oil*
- *1 ½ tbsp apple cider vinegar*
- *1 tsp salt or to taste*
- *2 tsp thyme*
- *1 tsp ground black pepper (optional)*

Directions

- Preheat the oven to 350 degrees F. Line the tray with parchment paper or aluminum foil.
- Wash and scrub the potatoes to clean and remove dirt. Leave the skin on and cut into 1-inch slices. Take each slice and cut it into sticks (about 1 inch by 1 inch by 4 inches). Put aside.

- Combine coconut oil and apple cider vinegar in a medium to a large bowl.
- Add the potato stems and add the oil and apple cider vinegar until fine. Add salt, thyme and pepper if you use it. Mix again, making sure the potatoes are well covered with the spices.
- Spread the fries on the prepared baking sheet in a single layer. Otherwise, they won't be crispy.
- Bake for 16-18 minutes or until tender. Let cool for 10 minutes.

NUTRITION FACTS (PER SERVING)

Calories	190	
Total Fat	7g	9%
Saturated Fat	6g	30%
Cholesterol	0mg	0%
Sodium	593mg	26%
Total Carbohydrate	29.7g	11%
Dietary Fiber	4.8g	17%
Total Sugars	2.2g	
Protein	3.2g	

<u>*Tips: Potatoes can be a great addition to your diet. They contain a good amount of fiber and nutrients, are also very filling and versatile. However, the way you prepare them can make a huge difference in terms of your diet – avoid frying them.*</u>

Greens Muffins

Prep time: 5 min | Cook time: 20 min | Servings: 4

Ingredients

- ½ cup coconut flour
- ½ cup rye flour
- ½ tsp salt
- ½ tsp baking powder
- ½ cup feta cheese
- ¾ cups coconut milk
- 2 eggs
- ½ tbsp coconut oil
- ⅛ cup yogurt
- ½ cup swish chard, chopped
- 1/2 can cardoon, drained and chopped

Directions

- Preheat the oven to 375 degrees F. You will need 12-cup muffin cups. In a large bowl, combine the flour, salt and baking powder.
- Add the feta cheese. Whisk coconut milk, eggs, oil and yogurt in a separate bowl.
- Make a well in the dry ingredients and add the milk and egg mixture, mixing with a spatula or wooden spoon until the dough comes together.
- Don't mix too much. Add the spinach and artichokes to the batter and mix gently.
- Line each muffin tin with a cupcake pan. Pour ¾ of the batter on the sides of each muffin pan. Bake for 15 minutes or until muffins have risen and tops are golden brown.

NUTRITION FACTS (PER SERVING)

Calories	318	
Total Fat	20.6g	26%
Saturated Fat	15.6g	78%
Cholesterol	99mg	33%
Sodium	553mg	24%
Total Carbohydrate	25.4g	9%
Dietary Fiber	10.7g	38%
Total Sugars	3.2g	
Protein	11.2g	

Tips: Swiss chard is a nutritional powerhouse - an excellent source of vitamins K, A and C, as well as a good source of magnesium, potassium, iron and fiber.

Tofu Quesadilla

Prep time: 5 min   Cook time: 20 min   Servings: 4

Ingredients

- 4 tsp coconut oil, divided
- 8 tbsp feta cheese, divided
- 8 (6-inch) rye tortillas
- 4 tsp minced onion, divided

For the Marinated Tofu

- ½ cup coconut aminos
- 2 tbsp maple syrup
- ½ cup chipotle in adobo, chopped
- 4 garlic cloves, sliced
- 8 ounces tofu

Directions

- In a small bowl, combine coconut aminos, maple syrup, chipotle adobo and ginger. Add the garlic and pour the dressing with the tempeh into a resealable plastic bag. Marinate in the refrigerator for at least 1 hour. The longer it is, the better. Bake, broil or fry until golden brown.
- Spread feta cheese evenly over 4 tortillas on a clean work surface, then sprinkle with onion and sliced tofu. Pour a tortilla over each.
- Heat 1 tsp of oil in a medium pan over medium-high heat. Add the assembled quesadillas to the pan and toss to brush with oil. Fry for 2 minutes, then flip and cook on the other side for another 2 minutes. Repeat with the other quesadilla.
- Serve with your favorite salsa.

NUTRITION FACTS (PER SERVING)

Calories	782	
Total Fat	48.2g	62%
Saturated Fat	17.8g	89%
Cholesterol	59mg	20%
Sodium	2027mg	88%
Total Carbohydrate	53.5g	19%
Dietary Fiber	4.5g	16%
Total Sugars	15.4g	
Protein	45.6g	

Tips: Tofu is a good source of protein and contains all nine essential amino acids. It is also a valuable plant source of iron and calcium as well as the minerals manganese and phosphorus. It also contains magnesium, copper, zinc and vitamin B1.

MAIN MEALS

Turkey Soup with Tarragon

Prep time: 5 min   Cook time: 20 min   Servings: 4

Ingredients

- *2 skinless turkey breast halves*
- *3 cups chicken broth*
- *2 cups water*
- *1 green onion, peeled*
- *1 clove*
- *1 bay leaf*
- *1 leek*
- *2 medium carrots, scrubbed and cut into small dice, 1 kept whole*
- *½ tsp black peppercorns*
- *1 tsp coconut oil*

- *1 small sweet potato, scrubbed and cut into a small dice*
- *1 small onion, peeled and finely diced*
- *Sea salt, to taste*
- *½ small bunch tarragon*

Directions

- Place the turkey in a large saucepan. Cover with water and bring to a boil over high heat. Once the turkey meat turns white, remove it and set it aside on a plate. Discard the water and foam that has formed and clean the pan.
- Return the turkey to the pot and cover with broth or cool water. Put the cloves in the green onion and place them in the pan with the bay leaf, the whole leek stalk, the whole carrot and the peppercorns. Simmer for 20 minutes.
- While the turkey cooks, heat the oil in a large casserole dish on medium-high. Add the chopped sweet potato, carrots, leek and onion and sprinkle with a little sea salt.
- Cook for 1 minute and cover. Reduce the heat to a low level and sweat the vegetables for about 8 minutes.
- Discard the green onion, vegetables and bay leaf from the pan with the turkey.
- Add the turkey and the broth to the vegetables. Simmer over very low heat for about 20 minutes. The chicken should be freshly cooked and the vegetables should be tender but not mushy. Try the salt.
- Turn off the heat and add the tarragon. Cover and let the pan sit for about 5 to 10 minutes for the flavors to develop.
- Remove the chicken from the soup, remove and discard the bones and thinly slice or mince the meat. Discard the bay leaf.
- Return the meat to the soup. Serve warm.

NUTRITION FACTS (PER SERVING)

Calories	203	
Total Fat	6.8g	9%
Saturated Fat	2.8g	14%
Cholesterol	60mg	20%
Sodium	943mg	41%
Total Carbohydrate	12.7g	5%
Dietary Fiber	2.3g	8%
Total Sugars	5.2g	
Protein	21.9g	

<u>Tips: Turkey has a high level of protein, B vitamins, selenium, zinc, and phosphorus as a popular meal. It can aid with a number of health problems such as muscle growth and maintenance due to its high level of vitamins.</u>

Acorn Squash Risotto

Prep time: 20 min Cook time: 20 min Servings: 8

Ingredients

- *2 tbsp avocado oil*
- *1 medium onion, chopped*
- *6 pounds Acorn squash seeded, peeled and cut into a 1-inch dice*
- *6 cups vegetable stock*
- *4 cups Arborio rice*
- *4 tbsp freshly grated Grana Padano cheese, or to taste*
- *4 tbsp butter, or to taste*
- *20 large, fresh Marjoram leaves, shredded*
- *Sea salt, to taste*

Directions

- Heat the avocado oil in a saucepan over medium heat.
- Add the onion, sprinkle with salt and cook, about 4 to 5 minutes, until it begins to soften. Add the Acorn squash, stir. Cover and sweat over medium heat for 8 minutes, stirring occasionally or until Acorn squash is tender.
- Add 4 cups of broth, bring to a boil and cover. Reduce the heat and simmer for 15 minutes, or until the Acorn squash is tender.
- Add the rice, stir to combine and cook for 15 minutes. The Acorn squash has crumbled and the rice is al dente.
- Add a little broth if it seems too thick. Add the Grana Padano. Salt to taste.
- While the rice cooks, melt the butter in a small saucepan or skillet over low heat. Do it slowly for the best results.
- When the butter has stopped frothing and is translucent with a brown nut residue, add the grated marjoram.
- Cook until crisp, about 2 minutes. Keep half of the leaves.
- Add the butter mixture to the rice. Cover and let stand for 2 minutes.
- Add some hot broth if the risotto seems dry; it must be a little thick.
- Sprinkle with reserved Marjoram leaves and a piece of grated Grana Padano cheese, and serve immediately.

NUTRITION FACTS (PER SERVING)		
Calories	384	
Total Fat	6.6g	8%
Saturated Fat	3.8g	19%
Cholesterol	15mg	5%
Sodium	138mg	6%
Total Carbohydrate	76.7g	28%
Dietary Fiber	7.2g	26%
Total Sugars	1.3g	
Protein	6.2g	

Tips: Acorn squash is high in antioxidants to be used to counteract damaging chemicals known as free radicals. These antioxidants can protect humans against diseases such as arthritis, cardiac illness, stroke, high blood pressure and certain types of cancer.

Green Onion & Quinoa Soup

Prep time: 30 min Cook time: 20 min Servings: 4

Ingredients

- 2 green onion, white parts only, washed and thinly sliced
- ½ parsnips, peeled cut into a small dice
- 1 tbsp coconut oil
- 3 cups of water or broth
- ¼ cup quinoa
- Salt, to taste
- Freshly grated goat cheese

Directions

- In a large, heavy-based saucepan, heat coconut oil over medium heat.
- Add the green onion, parsnips and 2 tbsp of water. Sprinkle with a little salt and sweat partially covered for 5 to 8 minutes or until the vegetables are tender.
- Add the remaining water. Lower the heat to medium-high and bring it to a boil. Add the quinoa and a generous pinch of salt.
- Bring the soup back to a boil, then cover the heat and reduce the heat to simmer for 20 minutes, stirring occasionally, until the quinoa is tender.
- Serve with plenty of freshly grated goat cheese.

NUTRITION FACTS (PER SERVING)

Calories	128	
Total Fat	5.4g	7%
Saturated Fat	1.3g	7%
Cholesterol	3mg	1%
Sodium	642mg	28%
Total Carbohydrate	13.8g	5%
Dietary Fiber	1.4g	5%
Total Sugars	2.7g	
Protein	6.2g	

Tips: A bland diet includes bland foods that are not very spicy and are low in fiber. If you are on a bland diet, avoid eating spicy, fried, or raw foods.

Marjoram & Lime Lamb Soup

Prep time: 30 min   Cook time: 40 min   Servings: 12

Ingredients

- *4 tsp coconut oil*
- *2 medium onions, chopped*
- *4 stalks leek, cut into ¼-inch dice*
- *4 medium parsnips, cut into ¼-inch dice*
- *Salt and pepper, to taste*
- *12 cups of water*
- *4 sprigs of marjoram*
- *2-inch lime peel*
- *40 ounces lamb on the bone*
- *1 cup quinoa*
- *1 tbsp lime juice*
- *2 tsp marjoram leaves chopped, for garnish*

Directions

- In a heavy-based saucepan with a lid, heat the olive oil over medium heat. Add the onions, leek, parsnip and a pinch of salt.
- Cook, 5 to 8 minutes, or until the onions are translucent, do not brown. Add the 6 cups of water, marjoram sprigs, lime zest and bone-in lamb. Bring to a boil, then simmer for at least 40 minutes to remove foam or grease from the surfaces.
- Add a little water when the soup has shrunk more than 1 inch.
- Remove the lamb and put it in a bowl, let it cool a bit, then chop the meat and discard the bones. Return the lamb to the soup, bring to a boil, then add the quinoa. Cook for 7 minutes then add the lime juice, season with the spices and turn off the heat.
- Arrange in bowls and serve with a pinch of fresh marjoram.

NUTRITION FACTS (PER SERVING)

Calories   145
Total Fat 8.1g   10%
Saturated Fat 2.2g   11%
Cholesterol 40mg   13%
Sodium 49mg   2%
Total Carbohydrate 8.2g   3%
Dietary Fiber 1g   4%
Total Sugars 1.6g
Protein 9.6g

Tips: Herbs may bring a bland diet to life. Dry herbs such as rosemary, thyme, fennel seeds, laurels and fresh herbs including parsley, marjoram, basil, mint and dill can be used.

Greens Soup

| Prep time: 20 min | Cook time: 40 min | Servings: 2 |

Ingredients

- ½ bunch arugula, well washed
- 1 tbsp butter
- ½ small onion, in a fine dice
- 1 cup chicken stock
- 1 cup water
- ½ cup frozen peas
- 2 cups baby spinach
- Sea salt to taste
- ½ tbsp basil

Directions

- Take the arugula and separate the thick, hard stems from the leaves. Keep the leaves and finely chop the stems.
- Over medium heat, heat the oil in a large pot or heavy-bottomed saucepan. Add the diced arugula stems and onion.

- Reduce heat to medium, sprinkle with salt and sauté until arugula and onion are tender but not dark, about five minutes.
- Add the broth, water and bring to a boil over medium heat. When the soup boils, reduce the heat to medium-low and simmer for 15 minutes.
- Add the frozen peas. Cook for two minutes or until tender. Add spinach and stir until they begin to wilt and turn a bright light green. To put out from heat.
- Blend the soup with a hand blender or in portions with a high-speed blender (for added safety, fill the vase halfway each time). Return the mixed soup to the pan and adjust seasonings as needed. When ready to serve hot, heat or refrigerate in the refrigerator. Serve with a tbsp of yogurt, chopped chives and croutons.

NUTRITION FACTS (PER SERVING)		
Calories	85	
Total Fat	4.4g	6%
Saturated Fat	0.7g	3%
Cholesterol	0mg	0%
Sodium	863mg	38%
Total Carbohydrate	8.9g	3%
Dietary Fiber	3g	11%
Total Sugars	3.8g	
Protein	3.7g	

Tips: Spinach is one of the healthiest leafy green vegetables. It contains essential nutrients. A cup of spinach provides you with protein, calcium, iron, magnesium, potassium, and vitamin A. You should add spinach to your daily diet.

Carrot Soup

Prep time: 20 min | Cook time: 55 min | Servings: 6

Ingredients

- *2 tbsp avocado oil*
- *1 onion, peeled and chopped*
- *salt and freshly ground black pepper*
- *1-pound carrots, peeled and sliced*
- *1 large sweet potato, peeled and diced*
- *wide strips of peel from ½ lime*
- *2 bay leaves*
- *6 cups vegetable stock or water*

Directions

- Heat the oil in a heavy-based saucepan over medium heat.
- Add the onion and cook, stirring occasionally, until tender but not golden, 8 to 10 minutes. Season with salt and pepper.
- Add the carrot, sweet potato, lime zest, bay leaves and 5 cups of vegetable broth. Cover the pot and cook, 30 to 45 minutes, until the vegetables are very tender.
- Discard the bay leaves. Reduce the soup in small amounts in a blender or food processor until very smooth. Add some of the remaining 1 cup of broth if the soup is too thick. Season with salt and pepper. Serve hot.

NUTRITION FACTS (PER SERVING)

Calories	88	
Total Fat	1.4g	2%
Saturated Fat	0.3g	1%
Cholesterol	0mg	0%
Sodium	141mg	6%
Total Carbohydrate	18.1g	7%
Dietary Fiber	4.5g	16%
Total Sugars	7.4g	
Protein	2.1g	

Tips: Freeze your soup to make it last and provide a quick last-minute meal. Simply double whatever recipe you are following. Cook all parts of the soup that need it, let it cool to room temperature, and then freeze!

Green Beans Risotto

Prep time: 45 min   Cook time: 40 min   Servings: 12

Ingredients

- 2 cups green beans
- 2 green onions
- 4 cups of stock
- 4 cups water
- 4 tbsp coconut oil
- 2 small onions, minced
- 6 tbsp chopped cilantro
- 3 cups arborio rice
- 6 tbsp freshly grated feta
- Sea salt, to taste

Directions

- Place the green beans, green onion and water and broth in a small saucepan.
- Bring to a boil, cover and bring to a boil. Cook for 20-30 minutes.

- Dip the green beans in the broth and water until they turn light green, about 1-2 minutes, then remove them with a colander. Keep to decorate, remove the broth from the heat.
- Heat coconut oil in a large saucepan over medium to high heat Add the onions and cook, stirring, until translucent. Don't let it turn brown. Add the cilantro and cook for 1 minute, then add the rice. Keep stirring.
- Add 1 tbsp of broth to the rice and cook, stirring, until absorbed. Add the broth 1 tsp at a time, reserve the last spoon and stir for about 15 to 20 minutes, until the rice is al dente and creamy. Add the green beans about halfway through cooking.
- Reduce the heat to medium-low and add the feta and butter, if using, and the last ladle of broth. Remove from the heat, cover and let stand for 5 minutes. Garnish with green beans tips and extra grated feta.

NUTRITION FACTS (PER SERVING)

Calories	740	
Total Fat	10.6g	14%
Saturated Fat	4.1g	20%
Cholesterol	15mg	5%
Sodium	201mg	9%
Total Carbohydrate	141.4g	51%
Dietary Fiber	5.5g	20%
Total Sugars	0.9g	
Protein	16.8g	

Tips: Green beans are high in vitamin K and also contain a decent amount of calcium. These nutrients are important for maintaining strong, healthy bones and reducing the risk of fractures.

Seafood Chowder

Prep time: 20 min   Cook time: 30 min   Servings: 4

Ingredients

- *1 lb. salmon, roughly chopped*
- *10 shrimps, peeled and deveined*
- *1 cup crab meat, chopped*
- *1 onion, diced*
- *1 daikon radish, peeled and chopped*
- *2 cups vegetable stock*
- *1 ½ cups full-fat coconut milk*
- *2 tbsp coconut oil*
- *sea salt and freshly ground black pepper*

Directions

- Heat the coconut oil in a large saucepan over medium heat.
- Add the shrimp to the pan and cook until pink, 2 to 3 minutes per side, set aside.
- Add the onion and garlic and cook, 3 to 4 minutes, stirring frequently.
- Place the chopped daikon in the pot and cook for 4 to 5 minutes.
- Add the salmon and cook for 2 to 3 minutes, add the vegetable stock and stir, scraping the bottom of the pan.
- Return the shrimp with the crab meat to the pot, cover and simmer for 12 to 15 minutes.
- Pour in the coconut milk and season to taste.

NUTRITION FACTS (PER SERVING)

Calories	337	
Total Fat	24.3g	31%
Saturated Fat	17.5g	87%
Cholesterol	113mg	38%
Sodium	180mg	8%
Total Carbohydrate	6.6g	2%
Dietary Fiber	2.1g	7%
Total Sugars	3.2g	
Protein	25.5g	

Tips: Slip the whole fillets into simmering chowder. This will cook them gently but no worries, they'll break apart in when cooked.

Roast Turkey

Prep time: 45 min | Cook time: 40 min | Servings: 8

Ingredients

- 1 whole turkey
- 1 tbsp coconut oil
- ½ medium lime
- 8 sprigs fresh rosemary
- Salt and pepper, to taste

Directions

- Preheat the oven to 400 degrees F.
- Remove all of the entrails from the inside of the turkey. Rinse the turkey under cold water. Pat dry with a paper towel. Remove excess fat from the body cavity. Rub the whole turkey with a little olive oil. Salt and pepper to taste.

- Place the turkey in a lightly greased roasting pan.
- Squeeze the lemon over the turkey and place the zest in the body cavity along with the 2 sprigs of rosemary. Place 4 of the remaining rosemary sprigs on the breast and tuck 2 in the folds between the legs and the body.
- Place the bird in the hot oven on a center shelf.
- Grill turkey 15 minutes per pound, plus 15 minutes at the end. For a 4-pound turkey, that would be 75 minutes.
- Occasionally brush the turkey with the juice that forms in the pan.
- When the cooking time is up, insert a skewer into the crease in the body of the thighs to verify that it is cooked through. The turkey is ready when the juices are clear and without traces of pink.
- Let turkey rest for 10 to 15 minutes, lightly covered with foil on the stovetop. This will make it juicier. After the bird has rested, there will be plenty of liquid in the pan.
- Use the liquid for the sauce. Here's how: Scrape off as much of the light fat from the top as possible and boil the rest of the sauce in a small saucepan. Season with salt to taste (if necessary).
- Cut the turkey into 8-10 pieces. Use turkey scissors when you have them, it's so much easier than cutting!
- Add the juice from the sculpture to the sauce. Serve with the hot sauce on a hot plate. Discard the skins if irritating.

NUTRITION FACTS (PER SERVING)

Calories	127	
Total Fat	9.4g	12%
Saturated Fat	3.7g	19%
Cholesterol	38mg	13%
Sodium	38mg	2%
Total Carbohydrate	1.2g	0%
Dietary Fiber	0.6g	2%
Total Sugars	0.1g	
Protein	9.4g	

Tips: Turkey is fairly comparable to chicken in terms of nutrients, but turkeys black and dark meat parts are leaner and contain fewer calories. Well-cooked or baked, turkey makes an ideal and easy to digest meal for a bland diet.

Beef and Vegetable Soup

Prep time: 15 min　　Cook time: 20 min　　Servings: 4

Ingredients

- *4 cups roast beef, shredded*
- *1 onion, chopped*
- *4 carrots, sliced*
- *1 sweet potato diced*
- *4 cups beef stock*
- *¼ cup coconut milk*
- *2 tbsp fresh chives, minced*
- *2 tbsp coconut oil*
- *sea salt to taste*

Directions

- In a large saucepan, heat the coconut oil over medium-high heat.
- Add the garlic and onion and cook, 2 to 3 minutes, until tender.
- Add the carrots and sweet potato to the pot and cook for another 2 to 3 minutes.
- Pour in the beef broth and bring to a boil.
- Bring to a boil and simmer for 15 to 20 minutes or until the vegetables are tender.
- Add the beef and cook until lukewarm.
- Add the coconut milk and season to taste.
- Serve warm and enjoy.

NUTRITION FACTS (PER SERVING)

Calories	232	
Total Fat	8.2g	11%
Saturated Fat	4.9g	25%
Cholesterol	61mg	20%
Sodium	717mg	31%
Total Carbohydrate	14.9g	5%
Dietary Fiber	3g	11%
Total Sugars	5.3g	
Protein	24.3g	

Tips: lean beef is rich in various vitamins and minerals, especially iron and zinc.

Pumpkin Soup

Prep time: 10 min | Cook time: 15 min | Servings: 6

Ingredients

- 1 tbsp coconut oil
- 1 medium onion, chopped
- 1 large carrot, chopped
- 1 leek, chopped
- 1 medium sized squash
- 3 cups vegetable broth
- 1 green apple, peeled, cored, and chopped
- 1 sprig fresh thyme
- 1 sprig fresh rosemary
- 1 tsp kosher salt
- ¼ tsp black peppercorns

Directions

- Choose to sauté in your Instant Pot. Add coconut oil and sauté onion, carrot, leek and garlic for about 3 to 5 minutes. Add the vegetable broth, pumpkin, apple, thyme, rosemary, salt, and pepper.
- Place the lid securely on the Instant Pot and turn the knob to close it. Cook under high pressure for 10 minutes and quickly release the pressure.
- Use a hand blender in the instant pot to puree the soup until smooth. If you don't have a hand blender, you can let the soup cool slightly and gently put it in a regular blender and stir until smooth.
- Serve the soup in bowls and serve lukewarm.

NUTRITION FACTS (PER SERVING)

Calories	142	
Total Fat	3.4g	4%
Saturated Fat	2.3g	11%
Cholesterol	0mg	0%
Sodium	784mg	34%
Total Carbohydrate	26.2g	10%
Dietary Fiber	3.3g	12%
Total Sugars	9.3g	
Protein	5.5g	

Tips: Since an Instant Pot shoots steam straight up, it's always best to use it in an unobstructed or well-circulated place, like under a hood vent. Avoid releasing steam right under cabinets – because repeated exposure to heat and steam can mess with wood and paint.

Sweet Potato & Thyme Risotto

Prep time: 20 min	Cook time: 40 min	Servings: 6

Ingredients

- 4 tbsp coconut oil
- 2 sprig fresh thyme
- 1 large yellow onion, diced
- 2 cup pearled barley
- 2 large sweet potatoes cut into a small dice
- 3 cups vegetable stock
- 3 cups water
- 2 tbsp freshly grated feta cheese (optional)
- 2 tsp butter (optional)
- Salt and pepper, to taste

Directions

- In a 5-liter casserole dish, heat coconut oil over medium-high heat.
- When it starts to curl, add the thyme and cook for a minute, then add the onions. Cook, stirring constantly, until the onions begin to turn transparent, about 2 minutes.
- Set the heat to medium, sprinkle the onions with a pinch of salt, stir and cover. Sweat for 8 minutes, stirring occasionally.
- Remove the lid, lower the heat to medium-high and add the barley. Mix and stir until the barley clicks against the side of the pan. Add the sweet potato and cook for another minute. Add the vegetable broth, water and bring to a boil. When the risotto has simmered, cover and lower the heat to low.
- Simmer for 20 minutes or until the barley is al dente and the sweet potatoes are tender. Stir in the feta and butter vigorously. This will break the sweet potatoes a bit.
- Cover, turn off the heat and let the risotto stand for 5 minutes. Check the salt and consistency.

NUTRITION FACTS (PER SERVING)		
Calories	401	
Total Fat	12g	15%
Saturated Fat	9.3g	47%
Cholesterol	6mg	2%
Sodium	101mg	4%
Total Carbohydrate	67.4g	25%
Dietary Fiber	13.3g	48%
Total Sugars	6g	
Protein	8.8g	

Tips: Sweet potatoes are often touted as healthier than white potatoes, but in reality, both types can be very nutritious. While potatoes and sweet potatoes are comparable in calories, protein, and carbohydrates, white potatoes provide more potassium, while sweet potatoes are incredibly high in vitamin A.

Coconut Parsnips Soup

| Prep time: 20 min | Cook time: 40 min | Servings: 2 |

Ingredients

- ½ tbsp coconut oil
- 1 small yellow onion, chopped
- 1 tsp red curry paste
- 1 tsp ginger powder
- 1 pound's parsnips, peeled and cut in into ½-inch pieces
- Salt, to taste
- 1½ cups water
- 1½ cups vegetable broth
- 1 cup coconut milk
- basil, for garnish

Directions

- In a medium saucepan, heat oil over medium to high heat. Add the onion and cook for 5 minutes or until translucent. Add the curry paste, ginger. Stir for 2 minutes.
- Add the parsnips and a generous pinch of salt. Cover the Parsnips and let them steam for 5 minutes, stirring occasionally. Cover and add water and broth and coconut milk. Bring to a boil. Cover and simmer for at least 30 minutes or until the carrots are tender.
- Puree the soup until very smooth. Heat and add more water if the soup is too thick. Serve with cilantro sprigs.

NUTRITION FACTS (PER SERVING)

Calories	384	
Total Fat	28.4g	36%
Saturated Fat	21.8g	109%
Cholesterol	0mg	0%
Sodium	914mg	40%
Total Carbohydrate	32.3g	12%
Dietary Fiber	8.4g	30%
Total Sugars	16.2g	
Protein	5.1g	

Tips: Coconut milk is slightly fatter than other plant-based milks, but the medium chain triglycerides (MCTs) in coconuts have been linked to certain heart health benefits, such as lower HDL cholesterol levels.

Baked Salmon with Quinoa

Prep time: 10 min   Cook time: 20 min   Servings: 4

Ingredients

- 4 (4 oz.) salmon fillets
- 1 cup quinoa
- 2 cups water
- 1 cup spinach, sliced
- 1 apple, cooked, peeled and cut into pieces
- ½ tsp salt
- ¼ tsp pepper
- fresh basil or cilantro for garnish

Directions

- Prepare quinoa. Put 1 cup of quinoa in a pot with 2 cups of water or boil 2 cups of water on the stove, add quinoa and salt. Simmer for about 30 to 35 minutes until the quinoa is tender.
- Preheat the oven to 400 degrees. Sprinkle the salmon with salt. Place on a baking sheet and bake for about 15-20 minutes.
- When the quinoa is ready, immediately stir in the spinach and cooked apple slices and season with salt to taste. Put the salmon over it.
- Garnish with basil or cilantro.

NUTRITION FACTS (PER SERVING)

Calories	315	
Total Fat	9.6g	12%
Saturated Fat	1.3g	7%
Cholesterol	50mg	17%
Sodium	351mg	15%
Total Carbohydrate	29.1g	11%
Dietary Fiber	3.7g	13%
Total Sugars	0.5g	
Protein	28.4g	

Tip: Chicken, beef or vegetable stock or broth can be substituted for water to add more flavor the quinoa.

DESSERT RECIPES

Almond Barley Pudding

Prep time: 20 min   Cook time: 40 min   Servings: 2

Ingredients

- 1 tsp nutmeg
- 2 cardamom pods
- ½ tsp Allspice
- ½ cup barley
- ¾ cup almond milk
- ¾ tbsp maple syrup
- toasted coconut (optional)

Directions

- Pour 2 cups of water, nutmeg, cardamom and Allspice into a medium saucepan.
- Heat over medium heat and bring the liquid to a boil.

- Add the barley after the liquid boils. Bring back to a boil and lower the heat. Bring the mixture to a boil. Cook for 15 to 20 minutes or until the rice is tender.
- Once the barley is cooked, turn off the heat and remove the cardamom.
- In another medium saucepan, heat the almond milk to a boil.
- Add maple syrup until combined. Then add the barley.
- Simmer the mixture for 7-9 minutes. The mixture thickens as the liquid evaporates. Remove from the heat when the desired consistency of the pudding is reached.
- Transfer to a bowl and garnish with toasted coconut.

NUTRITION FACTS (PER SERVING)

Calories	695	
Total Fat	48g	62%
Saturated Fat	42.2g	211%
Cholesterol	0mg	0%
Sodium	32mg	1%
Total Carbohydrate	64.8g	24%
Dietary Fiber	12.3g	44%
Total Sugars	14.7g	
Protein	8.5g	

Tips: Almond milk is a tasty and nutritious alternative to milk with many important health benefits. It is low in calories, low in sugar, and high in calcium, vitamin E, and vitamin D.

Plantain Baked

| Prep time: 20 min | Cook time: 40 min | Servings: 2 |

Ingredients

- *3 ripe Plantain bananas*
- *1½ tbsp butter*

Directions

- Preheat the oven to 425 degrees F. Line a baking sheet with parchment paper. Put aside.
- Melt the butter and pour it into a bowl or shallow plate.
- Peel the Plantain cut them at the top and bottom. Carefully cut it in half lengthwise. Roll in butter until well coated and place with cut surface down on a prepared baking sheet. Brush with the rest of the butter and rub a little nutmeg over it if desired.
- Cook on a high rack for 20 minutes.

- Gently flip the plantains with a spatula, do not break them, and bake for another 10 minutes, until golden brown with caramelized edges.
- Carefully remove them from the tray and serve hot with a tbsp of Greek yogurt.

NUTRITION FACTS (PER SERVING)		
Calories	438	
Total Fat	32.3g	41%
Saturated Fat	20.3g	101%
Cholesterol	84mg	28%
Sodium	227mg	10%
Total Carbohydrate	40.5g	15%
Dietary Fiber	4.6g	16%
Total Sugars	21.7g	
Protein	2.3g	

Tips: Plantains are suitable for the bland diet as they are easy to digest. They contain important antioxidants, vitamins and minerals. They are high in carbohydrates and a good source of fiber.

Sweet Potato Scones

| Prep time: 40 min | Cook time: 15 min | Servings: 6 |

Ingredients

- *1 cup rye flour*
- *¼ cup honey*
- *1 tsp baking powder*
- *⅛ tsp baking soda*
- *½ tsp Allspice*
- *¼ cup coconut oil*
- *¼ cup canned sweet potato puree*
- *⅛ cup buttermilk*

Directions

- Preheat the oven to 400 degrees F.
- Line a baking sheet with parchment paper.

- In a large bowl, combine the rye flour, honey, baking powder, baking powder, and Allspice.
- Cut the coconut oil into dry ingredients. Make a hole in the middle of the flour and coconut oil. Place the sweet potato puree and buttermilk in the center of the well. Incorporate the wet ingredients into the dry ingredients using a spatula, being careful not to over mix them.
- As soon as the dough is formed, pour over the floured part and form a rectangle about an inch thick. With a floured knife, cut a rectangle into 10-12 triangles and place it on a sheet of baking paper. Refrigerate rolls for 20 minutes.
- Bake the rolls for 10 to 12 minutes or until golden brown.

NUTRITION FACTS (PER SERVING)

Calories	197	
Total Fat	9.7g	12%
Saturated Fat	8g	40%
Cholesterol	0mg	0%
Sodium	35mg	2%
Total Carbohydrate	27.9g	10%
Dietary Fiber	5.2g	19%
Total Sugars	12.4g	
Protein	3.3g	

Tips: This dish makes a delicious, easy to digest, low in calories and nutritious dessert that children and adults will love.

Dairy-Free Rice Pudding

Prep time: 40 min   Cook time: 15 min   Servings: 6

Ingredients

- ½ cup rice
- ½ cup water
- 1½ cups unsweetened coconut milk
- 1 tsp nutmeg
- ¼ cup chopped fig
- ¼ cup maple syrup
- ½ tsp vanilla extract
- ½ cup sliced walnuts

Directions

- Put the rice in a colander and rinse with water. Drain for a few minutes.
- Put the rice in a large saucepan and add the water, coconut milk. Bring to a boil over medium heat.
- Simmer and cook for 30 minutes, stirring frequently to avoid sticking.
- Add the fig, maple syrup and vanilla extract. Stir to combine and remove from heat.
- Let cool to room temperature or put in a cool place. If the pudding gets too thick, add more coconut milk as needed.
- Serve with flaked walnuts.

NUTRITION FACTS (PER SERVING)

Calories	400	
Total Fat	11.2g	14%
Saturated Fat	1g	5%
Cholesterol	0mg	0%
Sodium	142mg	6%
Total Carbohydrate	69.6g	25%
Dietary Fiber	6.3g	22%
Total Sugars	34.6g	
Protein	9.9g	

Tips: Fiber can lower cholesterol and reduce the risk of heart disease and stroke. Since fiber will keep you full, it may be easier for you to maintain a healthy weight. Additionally, brown rice contains vitamins and minerals that help the blood carry oxygen and perform other vital functions.

Banana Quinoa

| Prep time: 15 min | Cook time: 0 min | Servings: 6 |

Ingredients

- 4 cups soy milk
- 2 cups quinoa
- 2 large ripe bananas, sliced
- 2 tsp honey
- ½ tsp ground nutmeg

Directions

- Put a saucepan on medium heat and add in the milk and bring to a boil.
- Add quinoa. Cook over medium heat for 1 to 2 minutes or until thickened, stirring occasionally.
- Add the banana, honey and nutmeg. Serve with more milk and nutmeg if desired.

NUTRITION FACTS (PER SERVING)

Calories	355	
Total Fat	6.5g	8%
Saturated Fat	0.8g	4%
Cholesterol	0mg	0%
Sodium	87mg	4%
Total Carbohydrate	61.7g	22%
Dietary Fiber	6.2g	22%
Total Sugars	16.6g	
Protein	13.9g	

Tips: The protein in soy milk is healthy, plant-based, and can help support healthy muscles and organs. Soy milk is high in omega-3 fatty acids, which are "healthy" fats that your body cannot make on its own.

Pumpkin Bread Pudding

Prep time: 40 min   Cook time: 15 min   Servings: 4

Ingredients

- 6 cups cubed rye bread
- 2 eggs
- ½ quart coconut milk
- ¼ tsp nutmeg
- ¼ tsp vanilla
- ¼ cup honey
- 1 cup roasted pumpkin, diced
- ⅛ cup raisins (optional)

Directions

- Preheat the oven to 350 degrees F.
- Butter a 9x13-inch glass baking dish.
- In a large bowl, combine the eggs, coconut milk, nutmeg, vanilla and honey.
- Place the bread in the bowl and stir until the bread is completely coated with liquid. Let the bread soak for at least 30 minutes.
- Add the pumpkin to the bread mixture. Stir in raisins if used.
- Place the bread in a baking dish. Bake for 40 to 60 minutes or until golden brown and firm.
- Serve with Greek yogurt or whipped cream, if desired.

NUTRITION FACTS (PER SERVING)

Calories	307	
Total Fat	4.8g	6%
Saturated Fat	2.2g	11%
Cholesterol	92mg	31%
Sodium	393mg	17%
Total Carbohydrate	52.9g	19%
Dietary Fiber	0.9g	3%
Total Sugars	17.9g	
Protein	7.3g	

Tips: Eating a healthy fiber diet can help lower your risk of colon cancer. With almost 3 grams of fiber in 1 cup of freshly baked pumpkin and over 7 grams in canned pumpkin, adding pumpkin to a daily diet can help a person increase their fiber intake while on a bland diet.

Coconut Avocado Pudding

Prep time: 40 min   Cook time: 15 min   Servings: 2

Ingredients

- *1 tbsp potato starch*
- *1 tbsp honey*
- *Pinch of salt*
- *¾ cups coconut milk*
- *1 egg yolk*
- *⅛ tsp vanilla extract*
- *½ ripe avocado*

Directions

- In a small, heavy-bottomed saucepan over the heat, combine the Potato starch, honey and a pinch of salt.
- Gradually add the coconut milk, making sure that no lumps form. Stir in the egg yolk and vanilla extract.
- Place the pot on medium heat and heat, stirring constantly, for 10 to 15 minutes until the mixture is thick and bubbly. To put out the fire.
- Peel and seed the avocado and mash it until very smooth. Add the lukewarm custard cream, season for sweetness, then transfer to a bowl, cover with cling film, and refrigerate for at least 1 hour.

NUTRITION FACTS (PER SERVING)

Calories	398	
Total Fat	33.5g	43%
Saturated Fat	21.9g	110%
Cholesterol	105mg	35%
Sodium	99mg	4%
Total Carbohydrate	24.2g	9%
Dietary Fiber	5.4g	19%
Total Sugars	12.2g	
Protein	4.4g	

Tips: Avocados are a great source of vitamins C, E, K, and B-6, as well as riboflavin, niacin, folic acid, pantothenic acid, magnesium, and potassium. They also provide lutein, beta-carotene, and omega-3 fatty acids. Most of an avocado's calories come from fat.

Yogurt Biscuits

| Prep time: 40 min | Cook time: 15 min | Servings: 6 |

Ingredients

- ½ cup low-fat Greek yogurt
- ⅛ cup almond milk
- 1½ cups rye flour
- ¼ cup maple syrup
- 2 tsp baking powder
- ½ tsp baking soda
- ½ tsp kosher salt
- ½ cup coconut oil

Directions

- Preheat the oven to 400 degrees F.
- Stir in yogurt with milk until smooth. Put aside.
- Combine flour, maple syrup, baking powder, salt and baking soda in a large mixing bowl.
- Rub the coconut oil into the dry ingredients between your fingers until the mixture resembles coarse flour. Add the yogurt mixture and stir with a wooden spoon until the mixture is evenly moist and a ball of dough begins to form.
- Add 1 tbsp of milk if it is too dry.
- Spread the dough with a dry measuring cup and place it on a baking sheet at a distance of 5 cm. Bake until golden brown, about 15 minutes. Transfer to a wire rack to cool.

NUTRITION FACTS (PER SERVING)

Calories	267	
Total Fat	12.3g	16%
Saturated Fat	7.5g	37%
Cholesterol	32mg	11%
Sodium	394mg	17%
Total Carbohydrate	35.2g	13%
Dietary Fiber	3g	11%
Total Sugars	12.4g	
Protein	4.1g	

Tips: Two cups of Greek yogurt a day can provide protein, calcium, iodine, and potassium and help you feel full on just a few calories. But perhaps more importantly, yogurt provides healthy bacteria for the digestive tract that can affect the entire body.

Pumpkin Pie Quinoa Pudding

| Prep time: 5 min | Cook time: 60 min | Servings: 2 |

Ingredients

- ½ cup quinoa
- 1 ¼ cup coconut milk, unsweetened
- ⅛ cup honey
- 1 tsp pumpkin pie spice (if tolerating)
- ¼ cup pumpkin puree

Directions

- Place quinoa, 1 cup of coconut milk, honey and pumpkin pie spice in a medium saucepan and place over high heat.
- Bring to a boil.
- After cooking, bring to a boil and cover. Simmer for 30 to 35 minutes. At this point, there should be some liquid left.
- Add 1 pumpkin puree and cook for another 10 to 20 minutes, or until the quinoa is cooked through and the consistency is thick. Add ¼ cup of coconut milk and mix.
- Serve hot.

NUTRITION FACTS (PER SERVING)

Calories	579	
Total Fat	38.5g	49%
Saturated Fat	32.1g	161%
Cholesterol	0mg	0%
Sodium	28mg	1%
Total Carbohydrate	56.1g	20%
Dietary Fiber	7.3g	26%
Total Sugars	23.5g	
Protein	9.9g	

Tips: Quinoa is one of the richest protein foods. It includes all nine necessary amino acids in its proteins. Quinoa consumption can lower your risk of acquiring hemorrhoids.

Granola

Prep time: 5 min   Cook time: 30 min   Servings: 9

Ingredients

- 6 cups barley
- 1 tbsp cinnamon
- ⅔ cup shredded unsweetened coconut
- 1 cup raw almonds, coarsely chopped
- 2 tbsp coconut oil
- ½ cup honey
- 1 cup dried cherries

Directions

- Preheat oven to 350 F. Coat a 9 "x 13" baking dish with cooking spray. Put aside.
- In a large bowl, combine the oats, cinnamon and coconut.
- Pour the oil and honey into a measuring cup. Microwave on HIGH for 30 seconds and stir it in the oat mixture.
- Pour the oatmeal mixture into the prepared pan. Bake for 30 minutes or until the oats are golden brown. Stir every 15 minutes to ensure even browning.
- Take the pan out of the oven. After cooling, add the dried cherries and mix well. Store in a tightly closed case.

NUTRITION FACTS (PER SERVING)

Calories	383	
Total Fat	13.9g	18%
Saturated Fat	5.4g	27%
Cholesterol	0mg	0%
Sodium	7mg	0%
Total Carbohydrate	58.5g	21%
Dietary Fiber	7.9g	28%
Total Sugars	16.8g	
Protein	9.7g	

Tips: Oats are among the healthiest grains on earth. They're a gluten-free whole grain and a great source of important vitamins, minerals, fiber and antioxidants.

Coconut Lemon Cake

| Prep time: 40 min | Cook time: 15 min | Servings: 6 |

Ingredients

- ½ cup rye flour
- ¼ tsp salt
- ¾ tsp baking powder
- ¼ cup butter, melted
- ¼ cup honey
- 2 large eggs, lightly beaten
- Grated peel of 1 lemon
- ⅓ cup dried coconut flakes, unsweetened
- Juice of 1 lemon

Directions

- Preheat the oven to 375 degrees F. Grease a 9 x 5 x 3-inch loaf pan with coconut oil. Put aside.
- Sift the flour, salt and baking powder into a bowl. Put aside.

- Combine honey and butter in a large bowl. When they are well mixed and light, beat the eggs one by one. Add the lemon zest then the grated coconut. Gradually sift the flour and stir it into the egg mixture until it is absorbed. The dough will be very loose.
- Pour the dough into the loaf pan and bake in the center of the oven until golden brown and a toothpick comes out clean, about 40 minutes. Let the cake rest in the pan for about 5 minutes, then tilt it on a wire rack to cool.
- While the cake is cooling, combine the lemon juice and the remaining 2 tbsp of honey in a small saucepan. Bring to a boil over medium heat until the sugar melts and forms a syrup with the juice.
- Put the cake on a plate, it will still be hot, and prick the top with a toothpick. Carefully pour the lime syrup over the cake and let it soak before adding the next tbsp. It runs down the sides of the cake.

NUTRITION FACTS (PER SERVING)

Calories	176	
Total Fat	11.3g	14%
Saturated Fat	8.9g	45%
Cholesterol	47mg	16%
Sodium	117mg	5%
Total Carbohydrate	17.8g	6%
Dietary Fiber	1.4g	5%
Total Sugars	8.7g	
Protein	2.7g	

Tips: High in fiber and MCTs, coconut can offer a number of benefits, including better heart health, weight loss, and digestion. However, it is high in calories and saturated fat, so it should be consumed in moderation.

Dulce de Leche Cookies

Prep time: 40 min   Cook time: 15 min   Servings: 6

Ingredients

- ½ cup coconut oil, melted
- ⅛ cup Greek yogurt, plain
- ¼ cup honey
- 1 large egg yolks
- ¾ tbsp orange zest
- ¼ tsp vanilla extract
- ¾ tsp rum extract
- ¼ cup rye flour
- ¼ cup sorghum flour
- ½ cup potato starch
- ½ tsp baking powder
- ¼ tsp salt

- 1 cup dulce de leche
- ¼ cup icing sugar

Directions

- In the bowl of an electric mixer, beat the coconut oil, yogurt and honey for 1 minute. Add the egg yolk, orange zest, vanilla extract and rum and mix well.
- Sift together rye flour, sorghum flour, potato starch, baking powder and salt. Add the flour mixture to the butter and stir over low heat until the dough comes together.
- Place the dough in a plastic bag and refrigerate for 30 minutes.
- Preheat the oven to 350 degrees F. Line two baking sheets with parchment paper and set aside.
- Take the dough out of the fridge and cut it in half. Place half of the dough on a lightly floured work surface. Roll out ¼ inch thick dough and cut 2-inch cookies with a round cookie cutter. Transfer the cookies to the prepared baking sheet. Mix the leftover dough with the other half of the dough and roll out the dough again to cut more cookies.
- Bake cookies for 10 minutes until lightly golden. Take out of the oven and let cool on the baking sheet.
- Spread about 1 ½ tsp of dulce de leche on the flat side of one cookie and sandwich on the flat side of another cookie. Repeat with the remaining cookies.
- Sprinkle the cookies with icing sugar and serve.

NUTRITION FACTS (PER SERVING)		
Calories	214	
Total Fat	8.6g	11%
Saturated Fat	5.2g	26%
Cholesterol	55mg	18%
Sodium	156mg	7%
Total Carbohydrate	32.7g	12%
Dietary Fiber	0.3g	1%
Total Sugars	8.6g	
Protein	1.5g	

Tips: Greek yogurt is made by draining the whey, which makes the yogurt thicker, creamier, and creamier, almost comparable to young cheese, but the freshness of taste and structure distinguishes it like yogurt. Real Greek yogurt is far fattier, containing up to 10% fat, whereas most of our yogurts include no more than 3.5 percent fat. Of course, you can find one with less fat on the shelves as well, which might come in handy while on a bland diet.

SMOOTHIES AND DRINKS

Banana Almond Smoothie

| Prep time: 10 min | Cook time: 00 min | Servings: 2 |

Ingredients

- 1½ cup almond milk
- 2 small frozen bananas
- 2 tsp maple syrup
- 4 ice cubes
- 4 tbsp water, as needed

Directions

- Put all the ingredients in a blender.
- Blend until smooth.
- Serve immediately and enjoy!

NUTRITION FACTS (PER SERVING)		
Calories	521	
Total Fat	43.3g	55%
Saturated Fat	38.2g	191%
Cholesterol	0mg	0%
Sodium	43mg	2%
Total Carbohydrate	37.5g	14%
Dietary Fiber	6.6g	24%
Total Sugars	22.3g	
Protein	5.2g	

Tips: Almond milk is a tasty and nutritious alternative to milk with many important health benefits. It is low in calories, low in sugar, and high in calcium, vitamin E, and vitamin D.

Plantains & Orange Smoothie

Prep time: 10 min	Cook time: 00 min	Servings: 2

Ingredients

- 1 banana
- ½ cup orange juice (in tolerating)
- ⅛ cup almond milk
- 2 scoops protein powder
- ½ tbsp maple syrup
- 1 cup ice

Directions

- Put all the ingredients in a blender.
- Blend until smooth.
- Serve immediately and enjoy!

NUTRITION FACTS (PER SERVING)		
Calories	260	
Total Fat	5.9g	8%
Saturated Fat	4.2g	21%
Cholesterol	65mg	22%
Sodium	63mg	3%
Total Carbohydrate	30.6g	11%
Dietary Fiber	2.7g	10%
Total Sugars	18.6g	
Protein	23.8g	

Tips: Bananas are one of the most popular fruits in the world. They include very important nutrients, but overeating could end up doing more harm than good. Too much of one food can contribute to weight gain and nutritional deficiencies.

Chocolate Coconut Smoothie

Prep time: 10 min | Cook time: 00 min | Servings: 2

Ingredients

- ¼ cup hemp seeds, crushed
- ¼ cup coconut oil, melted
- ¼ cup canned coconut milk
- ⅛ cup cocoa powder
- ⅛ cup maple syrup
- ½ cup unsweetened soy milk

Directions

- Put all the ingredients in a blender.
- Blend until smooth.
- Serve immediately and enjoy!

NUTRITION FACTS (PER SERVING)		
Calories	484	
Total Fat	43.1g	55%
Saturated Fat	30.9g	154%
Cholesterol	0mg	0%
Sodium	39mg	2%
Total Carbohydrate	22.7g	8%
Dietary Fiber	3.1g	11%
Total Sugars	15.3g	
Protein	8.7g	

Tips: Just 2-3 tbsp of these hemp hearts can give your diet a nutritional boost. You can mix them into smoothies and shakes or even make milk out of them, which might be handy while on a bland diet. You can add them to rice, salads, fruit bowls, khichdi, pasta, smoothies or juices.

Apple Pie Smoothie

Prep time: 10 min   Cook time: 00 min   Servings: 1

Ingredients

- ¼ cup mashed banana
- 6 tbsp plain Greek yogurt
- ½ tsp allspice powder (if tolerating)
- ½ tsp honey, or to taste
- 1½ tbsp apple juice or water, as needed

Directions

- Put all the ingredients in a blender.
- Blend until smooth.
- Serve immediately and enjoy!

NUTRITION FACTS (PER SERVING)		
Calories	236	
Total Fat	1g	1%
Saturated Fat	0.5g	2%
Cholesterol	3mg	1%
Sodium	29mg	1%
Total Carbohydrate	55.3g	20%
Dietary Fiber	2g	7%
Total Sugars	44.3g	
Protein	3.7g	

Tips: Apples are rich in fiber, vitamins, and minerals, all of which are good for you. They also provide a wide variety of antioxidants. These substances help neutralize free radicals. Free radicals are reactive molecules that can build up through natural processes and environmental influences.

Avocado Smoothie

| Prep time: 5 min | Cook time: 0 min | Servings: 1 |

Ingredients

- *1 avocado*
- *2 medium bananas*
- *2 cups kale*
- *2 cup coconut milk*
- *1tsp honey (optional)*

Directions

- Put all ingredients into a blender
- Blend until smooth.
- Serve and enjoy!

NUTRITION FACTS (PER SERVING)		
Calories	479	
Total Fat	32g	41%
Saturated Fat	14.2g	71%
Cholesterol	0mg	0%
Sodium	65mg	3%
Total Carbohydrate	48.3g	18%
Dietary Fiber	10.8g	39%
Total Sugars	17.8g	
Protein	6.6g	

Tips: Bananas have a high level of iron; therefore, consumption can boost blood hemoglobin production. In addition, bananas are also easy to digest.

Healthy Shamrock Shake

| Prep time: 10 min | Cook time: 00 min | Servings: 1 |

Ingredients

- 1 cup Swiss chard
- ⅛ tsp peppermint extract
- 1½ tbsp vanilla protein powder
- ⅛ cup low fat cream
- ½ cup coconut milk
- ½ tsp maple syrup
- 1 cup ice

Directions

- Put all the ingredients in a blender.
- Blend until smooth.
- Serve immediately and enjoy!

NUTRITION FACTS (PER SERVING)		
Calories	495	
Total Fat	35g	45%
Saturated Fat	28.8g	144%
Cholesterol	36mg	12%
Sodium	198mg	9%
Total Carbohydrate	13.7g	5%
Dietary Fiber	3.2g	12%
Total Sugars	8g	
Protein	38.2g	

Tips: Swiss chard is a nutritional powerhouse - an excellent source of vitamins K, A and C, as well as a good source of magnesium, potassium, iron and fiber.

Hot Chocolate

| Prep time: 10 min | Cook time: 00 min | Servings: 1 |

Ingredients

- 2 cups almond milk
- 1 tbsp chocolate protein powder
- 1½ tbsp cocoa powder
- ⅛ cup maple syrup

Directions

- Put all the ingredients in a blender.
- Blend until smooth.
- Serve immediately and enjoy!

NUTRITION FACTS (PER SERVING)		
Calories	469	
Total Fat	17.5g	22%
Saturated Fat	9.3g	47%
Cholesterol	50mg	17%
Sodium	194mg	8%
Total Carbohydrate	66.7g	24%
Dietary Fiber	10.6g	38%
Total Sugars	44g	
Protein	29.4g	

Tips: Protein powder is in general safe for most children and adults if taken correctly. High doses can cause side effects such as increased stools, nausea, thirst, gas, cramps, loss of appetite, fatigue (fatigue) and headache.

Apple Compote Smoothie

Prep time: 10 min | Cook time: 00 min | Servings: 1

Ingredients

- ¼ apple puree
- 6 tbsp plain yogurt
- 1 tbsp honey
- ⅛ tsp nutmeg
- ¼ tsp vanilla extract
- ⅛ cup cooked quinoa
- coconut milk, as needed
- A few ice cubes

Directions

- Put all the ingredients in a blender.
- Blend until smooth.
- Serve immediately and enjoy!

NUTRITION FACTS (PER SERVING)		
Calories	267	
total Fat	6.2g	8%
Saturated Fat	4.3g	22%
Cholesterol	6mg	2%
Sodium	69mg	3%
Total Carbohydrate	43.8g	16%
Dietary Fiber	2.8g	10%
Total Sugars	28g	
Protein	8.9g	

Tips: You can make your apple pure by way of cooking your apples, skinless and seedless, with a sprinkle of sugar or cinnamon, until tender, about 15 minutes. Once soft and tender, drain the liquid to a separate bowl and keep it (it makes a great warm apple juice) while you bland the apples until well combined.

Cantaloupe Smoothie

Prep time: 10 min　　Cook time: 0 min　　Servings: 1

Ingredients

- ½ cantaloupe
- 1 cup coconut milk
- 1 ½ cups ice

Directions

- Place all ingredients in a high-speed blender.
- Blend until smooth.

NUTRITION FACTS (PER SERVING)

Calories	212	
Total Fat	20.1g	26%
Saturated Fat	18g	90%
Cholesterol	0mg	0%
Sodium	61mg	3%
Total Carbohydrate	8.8g	3%
Dietary Fiber	0.3g	1%
Total Sugars	4.7g	
Protein	1.3g	

Tips: Cantaloupe contains several ingredients - fiber, potassium, and vitamin C - that contribute to keeping our heart healthy. Food high in fiber help control blood pressure and lower LDL and bad cholesterol.

Chai Tea Smoothie

Prep time: 10 min | Cook time: 0 min | Servings: 2

Ingredients

- *1 cup unsweetened coconut*
- *1 chai teabag*
- *1 very ripe frozen banana, cut into chunks*
- *¼ teaspoon pure vanilla extract*

Directions

- In a small saucepan on the stovetop, heat the milk in for a minute or two, until hot and starting to boil.
- Put the teabag in the milk and put it in the refrigerator until it cools.
- Combine the tea-infused milk, banana and vanilla in a blender and blend until smooth.

NUTRITION FACTS (PER SERVING)

Calories	108	
Total Fat	0.4g	1%
Saturated Fat	0.1g	1%
Cholesterol	0mg	0%
Sodium	1mg	0%
Total Carbohydrate	27.1g	10%
Dietary Fiber	3.1g	11%
Total Sugars	14.6g	
Protein	1.3g	

<u>Tips: While they make a fantastic healthy breakfast or snack throughout the day, smoothies are not a good idea before bedtime.</u>

Ginger Butter Squash Latte

| Prep time: 10 min | Cook time: 00 min | Servings: 1 |

Ingredients

- ½ (15 oz) can sweet potato puree
- 1 cup coconut milk
- 1½ tbsp honey, to taste
- ½ tsp pumpkin pie spice
- 2 shots espresso
- Whipped cream for garnish

Directions

- Put all the ingredients in a blender.
- Blend until smooth.
- Serve immediately and enjoy!

NUTRITION FACTS (PER SERVING)		
Calories	490	
Total Fat	28.8g	37%
Saturated Fat	25.5g	127%
Cholesterol	0mg	0%
Sodium	43mg	2%
Total Carbohydrate	62.7g	23%
Dietary Fiber	3.3g	12%
Total Sugars	55g	
Protein	3.7g	

Tips: Sweet potatoes in your daily diet can meet your body's vitamin and mineral needs and help improve eyesight, control blood pressure and sugar levels, and reduce the risk of a stroke.

Red Velvet Smoothie

| Prep time: 10 min | Cook time: 0 min | Servings: 2 |

Ingredients

- *1 beet, cooked and sliced*
- *½ banana*
- *1 cup low-fat coconut milk*
- *crushed ice*

Directions

- Place all ingredients in a high-speed blender.
- Blend until smooth.

NUTRITION FACTS (PER SERVING)		
Calories	334	
Total Fat	29.4g	38%
Saturated Fat	25.9g	130%
Cholesterol	0mg	0%
Sodium	59mg	3%
Total Carbohydrate	19.4g	7%
Dietary Fiber	4.5g	16%
Total Sugars	12.2g	
Protein	4.1g	

Tips: Beetroots contain a lot of nutrients. They are a great source of fiber, vitamin B9, potassium, iron, and vitamin C. They are associated with numerous health benefits, such as improved blood flow, lower blood pressure, and increased exercise performance.

2-WEEKS MEAL PLAN

1st Week Meal Plan

Day	Breakfast	Snack	Lunch	Dinner	Dessert
1	Kale and Cheese Omelette	Banana Almond Smoothie	Roast Turkey	Greens Soup	Dairy-Free Rice Pudding
2	Apple Pie Smoothie	Berry Pancakes	Marinated Tempeh	Green Beans Risotto	Granola
3	Savory Potato Fries	Kiwi Slushie	Turkey Soup with Tarragon	Sweet Potato & Thyme Risotto	Sweet Potato Scones
4	Almond Barley Pudding	Healthy Shamrock Shake	Green Beans Risotto	Coconut Parsnips Soup	Coconut Lemon Cake
5	Scrambled Eggs	Chocolate Coconut Smoothie	Coconut Parsnips Soup	Marinated Tempeh	Coconut Lemon Cake
6	Dairy-Free Rice Pudding	Plantains, Orange & Strawberry Smoothie	Marjoram & Lime Lamb Soup	Green Onion & Quinoa Soup	Pumpkin Bread Pudding
7	Greens Muffins	Apple Pie Smoothie	Roast Turkey	Acorn Squash Risotto	Plantain Baked

2nd Week Meal Plan

Day	Breakfast	Snack	Lunch	Dinner	Dessert
1	Tofu Quesadilla	Kiwi Slushie	Greens Soup	Coconut Parsnips Soup	Banana Pancakes
2	Kale & Cheese Omelette	Granola	Marinated Tempeh	Turkey Soup with Tarragon	Yogurt Biscuits
3	Berry Pancakes	Ginger Butter Squash Latte	Frittata with Leafy Greens	Roast Turkey	Coconut Lemon Cake
4	Apricots & Quinoa Porridge	Apple Pie Smoothie	Sweet Potato & thyme Risotto	Green Beans Risotto	Coconut Avocado Pudding
5	Fruity and Healthy Barley	Shamrock Shake	Green Onion & Quinoa Soup	Green Onion & Quinoa Soup	Plantain Baked
6	Banana Pancakes	Hot Chocolate	Roast Turkey	Acorn Squash Risotto	Pumpkin Bread Pudding
7	Greens Muffins	Banana Almond Smoothie	Coconut Parsnips Soup	Marjoram & Lime Lamb Soup	Almond Barley Pudding

Made in the USA
Monee, IL
11 December 2021